MW01245045

10 STEPS TO GET OVER YOUR EX LOVER

LOVE MONEY AND FITNESS TO A BETTER YOU

MADISON HILTON

CO AUTHOR, LAMONT HOLLIDAY

Copyright © 2018. All Rights Reserved.

No part of this publication may be reproduced, distributed, or transmitted in any form or by any means, including photocopying, recording, or other electronic or mechanical methods, or by any information storage and retrieval system without the prior written permission of the publisher, except in the case of very brief quotations embodied in critical reviews and certain other noncommercial uses permitted by copyright law.

For more information on upcoming free books email me your email address at

lamontholliday@gmail.com

WHY YOU SHOULD READ THIS BOOK

It's over--and it really hurts. But as unbelievable as it may seem when you are in the throes of heartache, you can move past your breakup. Forget about trying to win your ex back. Forget about losing yourself and trying to make this person love you. Starting today, this breakup is the best time to change your life for the better, inside and out.

I've had my share of relationships end that left me paralyzed in pain. I remember lying in bed for weeks crying myself to sleep thinking that the pain was going to end eventually when my ex came to his senses. I know that during that time I also hurt a lot of people close to me because not only did I not want their help, I may have treated them harshly for not understanding what I was going through. I know how that pain can cause you to do things that are completely out of your element, and I know you will look back in time and wonder how exactly you made it through those times. I have experienced this pain more than once, and my journey can offer you a unique perspective that can help to gain back control of your life.

Getting over an ex is a difficult thing to do, and once you have decided to move on you really need someone to help who has been there before to offer helpful advice.

TABLE OF CONTENTS

INTRODUCTION

Going through a breakup is tough. I can tell that from personal experience. It can be like trying to ride a bicycle up a mountain. You should pedal hard, or else you will be dragged back down. If you are not careful, you will lose your balance and fall again. If you were in a good and happy relationship that went on for a long time, the feeling of separation can be nerve-wreaking. It may seem very tough to get through. You will have a range of emotions from pain, fear, frustration and disappointment. But life must go on. You must gather yourself and come back to the mainstream and live your life. In time things will be better. This said, you cannot relax and wait for things to get better. You have to make things happen and there is no doubt that things will indeed get better.

So, the break up was unavoidable. Now you are desperate for a way to forget your ex, the one person that you still love so much, who has torn your heart apart. Anything you do, you see and you hear remind you of them, and how things used to be, and how wrong this break up was. So what is the best way to forget them and pretend nothing has happened?

Unfortunately, there is no magic pills that could do that. Like it or not, you have to go through the painful process. Most of us have been there, and we survived, so you will too. The hard part is to accept. What has happened cannot be undone. But there is a good news. Human feelings are temporary. You may feel like your world has crumbled to pieces, but in a week time, you will actually feel less pain. Maybe in a few months' time you would laugh yourself silly for crying in self-pity like this. You just have to go through the process, like everyone else.

Therefore, instead of wondering how to actually forget the one you love, which is not going to happen anyway, let's focus on how to lessen the pain and learn something useful out of the experience so that you don't make similar mistakes in the future. Try to use your head instead of your heart. Nothing seems fair, but you need to keep going and make a wise decision. Put yourself as an outsider who looks into the situation from outside the box. If this happened to your best friend, what kind of advice would you give them?

After a breakup, you feel as if you are in a wild rainforest. You feel lost, cold, and completely helpless. But you don't have to feel this way! Breaking up survival is not an alien concept for those you have been in and out of relationships. Yes, you can find your way through the confusion and survive.

Breaking up survival is no different from trying to survive in a remote forest where you are hours and miles away from civilization. The first thing you need is to find a safe spot to keep you out of harm's way: hang-out with your girlfriends, get out of your house and try to get some fresh air!

Other important things that you would need written in our imaginary breaking up survival rulebook are that you have to have fire and water. Fire to keep you warm, and water to keep you alive. Whatever you think could be equal to fire and water - shopping, drinking, eating ice cream, having a DVD marathon - you go ahead and get it or do it.

Do whatever you can to make yourself feel better, because while it is normal to feel sadness after a breakup, breaking up survival means that you have to fight and fight until you can say that you can stand on your own feet once again, to face the world and all that it has to offer.

Breaking up, as the Beatles one sang, is hard to do, and it becomes harder if the relationship you ended has been a long and serious one. There is no guidebook on breaking up survival: it is one thing that those who have survived before us can teach us.

But just because heartbreak may feel like the end of the world, the good news is the pain won't last forever - and it certainly won't keep you from falling in love again.

Breaking up is tough to deal with but it's even more so when someone has been spurned in a relationship with what seems no way to get back in. In most circumstances, using a shoulder is the instinctive thing to do but after the initial meeting, the majority of people you hang out with will tire quickly of hearing about your problems and you suddenly find people will start to avoid you.

What happens next is you begin to feel lonelier than ever and feel like you are being excluded from certain activities simply because friends and family know you are hurting but want to avoid the doom and gloom and while they try to be nice about it, it usually hurts even more.

I've seen friends and relatives break up and be miserable about it. I've heard them saying, "I don't want them back" or "I want to get over this pain" but I'd often caught them spying their exes on their social network pages or just suddenly remembering the good times they have.

The hardest thing about "getting over" someone is that in order to move on, we have to figure out what we're actually grieving. Whenever we go through a breakup, we don't just break up with our partner—we also break up with our future. By that I mean, the future we had imagined taking place with this person. And when we're grieving the loss of our past and our future, it's hard to stay in the present—and do something to improve it.

Therapists talk a lot about how the past informs the present—how our histories affect the ways we think, feel, and behave, and how at some point in our lives we have to let go of the fantasy of changing the past, or else we remain stuck. Changing our relationship to our pasts is a staple of therapy. But we talk far less about how our relationship to the future informs the present. Our struggle to release a wished-for future can be just as powerful a roadblock to change as our struggle to release a wished-for past.

It may seem like you're completely focused on the present—specifically, getting your ex out of your head now—but because so much of your fixation with him involves thinking about the relationship you used to have and the relationship you want with him going forward, you're toggling between past and future without actually living in the present. Once you anchor yourself in the present, though, you'll be able to accept the loss of your longed-for future so that you can create a new one.

This anchoring might begin by considering why you're currently investing so much emotional real estate in a person you can't have—a person who, even when you were in the relationship, didn't share the desire for the future you wanted. You say that your ex was "the last person I had the strongest romantic relationship and potential with," but how strong can the potential have been with a person who doesn't reciprocate the connection you're seeking? Most important, is it possible that you haven't found the connection you're looking for in the present because you aren't, in fact, open to men who might love you the way you want to be loved?

As painful as it is to not be able to have your ex, I think that in some ways it's his distance—his occasional appearance without really getting too close—that keeps you emotionally tied to him, because something about that distance probably feels familiar, like home. Most of us are drawn to romantic partners because our unconscious pulls us toward the familiar—the characteristics of whoever cared for us growing up, even if they made us feel edgy or confused or unseen (like your ex does). It's no coincidence that people who had angry parents often end up choosing angry partners; or that those with alcoholic parents might be drawn to partners who drink quite a bit; or that those who had distant or critical parents find themselves married to somebody distant or critical.

Why would people do this to themselves? It's certainly not intentional. In the beginning of a relationship, these characteristics may be barely perceptible and often the person seems very different from our parents, but our unconscious has finely tuned radar inaccessible to our conscious mind. It's not that we want to get hurt again—it's that we want to master a situation in which we felt helpless as a child. Freud called this "repetition compulsion." Maybe this time, a part of you imagines, I can go back and heal that wound from long ago by engaging with somebody familiar—but new. The only problem is, by choosing the familiar partner, we guarantee the opposite result: We reopen the wound and feel even more inadequate and unlovable.

It's natural to miss your ex but if the break up has happened for quite a long time and that ex has really moved on, I think it's about time to really move on from that relationship and start getting over that ex.

According to research published in The Journal of Positive Psychology, it takes 11 weeks to feel better after a relationship ends. But a separate study found it takes closer to 18 months to heal from the end of a marriage.

In reality, heartbreak is a grieving process - and it looks completely different for everyone.

Because love is a messy emotion, and each relationship comes with its own memories and feelings, the end of any relationship will be a unique experience.

And there is no set time limit for healing - as factors including the length of the relationship, shared experiences and memories, whether you had children, betrayal, and the depth of emotion all play a part in the healing process.

The break-up can also be worse or more painful if you didn't want the relationship to end.

Fortunately, although it may not seem like it in the moment, millions of other people are experiencing similar emotions - and millions more have.

Human beings are meant to form relationships and fall in love. And just as most people will experience love at least once in their lifetime, many will also experience the sting of heartbreak. It is natural, and expected, to be upset and devastated at the end of a relationship - even when the relationship might not have been a positive thing. After all, love is blind and it has the ability to make people overlook their partner's flaws. This is truest at the end of a relationship, when bad memories are often overshadowed by good ones that make us question why we broke up in the first place.

But, just like any other wound, heartbreak heals with time, self-care, and a positive outlook - and it is possible to move on.

And while no two relationships are alike, there are certain things that everyone suffering from heartbreak can do to move on. In the subsequent chapters, we will show you 10 practicable ways to get over your ex easily and live a life you have always deserved.

Please leave a review on Amazon !!!

Thanks ,Lamont

CHAPTER 1

STAY SINGLE

Why is it that some people want to stay single for the rest of their lives? Well, some people say that being single is a simple way of living a happy life. They say that those who choose to stay single lead uncomplicated lives. You can make your own decisions without having to consult anyone. You can do what you want to do with your life without any interference from other people.

But most people who stay single, have their reasons for doing so. One of these is that they have been unable to find the perfect partner with whom they can commit themselves and share the rest of their lives. They do not want to experience the bitterness and the heartaches they experienced in their previous relationships. They are afraid to commit to another relationship because for them, it is safer to stay single. Afraid to make a commitment is another reason why some want to stay single. They call it commitment-phobic. They are just afraid to entrust themselves in a deeper commitment and they don't want to take the risk where they feel that their singleness is at stake. They just feel that they just cannot give in to the demands of others and they are already contented with their lives.

Sometimes, these people spend a lot of time looking for a person who will meet their standards. And with all the frustrations and disappointments they have experienced in searching for that perfect someone, they just decide to stay single.

There are many reasons to take time alone before getting into the next relationship. Ultimately, we need time to figure out what we want out of life and who we are as individuals before we can determine who might be a good fit for us as a partner, and before we can fully and genuinely give ourselves to another person.

When my last relationship ended, I vowed to myself that I would be single for at least a year before getting involved again. That relationship came at the heels of a 6-year long relationship with someone I still truly adore, but from whom I had grown apart and we were no longer right for each other. I never doubted that ending it was the right thing to do, but it was still a painful break.

Although I've never been one to get seriously involved with a rebound, it turns out, I'm only human. The relationship that evolved from that rebound was ill-conceived from the start. It was stressful, tumultuous and often contentious. Neither of us treated the other with the respect we should have and yet, I still felt stuck in it, in part, because I had not done the hard work I needed to have done before the relationship started. When I finally broke free of that relationship, I'm happy to say I stuck to my vow to remain single for at least a year, and I can't tell you how grateful I am. There's probably nothing magical about hitting the one year mark, but for me, in that situation, it's what felt right.

As a therapist in private practice in Paterson New Jersey, concerning relationships, breakups and divorces tend to be one of the main causes of stress in people's lives. Even when people know better, they often get involved in the wrong relationship or stay in for too long, because breakups can be extremely destabilizing for even the most stable people.

We all feel lonely when a relationship ends. No matter how bad the relationship was, most people miss the sense of companionship that their ex provided during the good times. There might be an impulse to grab onto the first person we find who might be a remotely suitable partner. But it's important to take a step back and examine our lives a bit first.

When we rush too quickly into a relationship, we are usually not ready to enter into it in an emotionally healthy way, and we also tend to make very poor choices about whom we get involved with. Once your life has re-stabilized after that tough breakup and you're OK being on your own, you will be able to see a potential partner much more clearly, rather than grasping for someone else simply because you're lonely or you fear you won't find someone better.

Once you've realized the relationship you're in isn't serving you the way it should be, here are some tips to help you move on in the healthiest way possible. Not everyone will necessarily need to take all of these steps (though some will need to), but these are some of the most common obstacles I see people struggle with when they end, or consider starting, a relationship. I recommend considering each one for at least a moment to determine if it might be helpful to you. Be thoughtful and be honest with yourself.

First, figure out who you are now that the last relationship is done and what you want out of life moving forward.

Over time, we all change and evolve – especially in our 20s, but all throughout adulthood as well. That process of change is natural, healthy and important for us to experience. Sometimes people who are in committed relationships can't see that change quite as clearly as people who are single.

Even the most introspective and enlightened people see themselves differently when they're in relationships. No matter how independent you might be, when you're in a relationship, you see yourself in relationship to your partner on many different levels. That's part of being human and it's part of having a healthy, collaborative relationship. No matter how much you might meditate, journal or talk to your therapist, you still need time to see what your life is like without that other person in it or on your mind every day before you can start to see who you are without them.

This means that it's not enough to simply spend time without your ex, you actually have to let go and get them off your mind. Unfortunately, the best cure for this is usually time. And that time helps you start to see your own life a bit more clearly. Even after you've let go of your ex, you still need time to live life from this new perspective for a while and see what it's like.

How have you changed since your last relationship started? How has your life changed? Your circumstances? What do you really want out of life now that you've made those changes? What are your goals, dreams and limitations? Where and how does a partner fit into those things?

Many of these things might have changed a lot more than you realize so take the time to really think about it before getting involved with a partner whose life and goals might not fit well with yours.

Figure out what you want from your next relationship.

Now that you've figured out whom you are and how you want your life to be, you can start to think about what your ideal partner would be like.

Make a list of things about your ideal partner that includes the following about the person: required qualities, ideal qualities that might be negotiable, red flag warning signs, absolute deal breakers. For example, things like being kind, compassionate and compatible might be requirements, whereas being tall or speaking another language might be ideal qualities that you would like your partner to have but you can live without.

Disrespectful treatment might be a deal breaker for you, and being evasive or cryptic about things might be a red flag that the person isn't being honest with you. You might also notice that the person is always kind to you but not kind to others, and this might be a red flag that the person isn't being sincere with you and over time, they will be less kind.

These are just examples, and you will have to create your own list. Put some time into it, and make the list before you meet someone new, so that you can really think about it objectively rather than trying to make it fit the person you're seeing.

Become a healthy, stable, whole person on your own first.

A healthy relationship is made up of two healthy people. It might sound cliché, but it's true that we can't truly love another person if we haven't accepted ourselves for who we are. If we don't truly love ourselves, then we enter relationships from a place of needing the other person in some way, rather than wanting to be with them because we love them and want to offer ourselves to them.

It's only when we truly love and accept ourselves and feel whole and happy on our own that we can give ourselves fully to another person. When we have emotional stability and self-respect, then we can navigate through relationships with respect, both for ourselves and for the other person. Without that self-respect, we're likely to encounter drama, clinginess, codependence, jealousy and other trust issues.

Remember, the relationship can only be as healthy as the least healthy person in it. If you're not in a good place, the relationship will reflect that. If you rely too heavily on your partner to make you happy or feel fulfilled, that will eventually put too great a burden on both your partner and on your relationship. External factors, including other people, cannot make you happy, so if you want to have a healthy and successful relationship, you need to be happy and healthy on your own first, before entering into the relationship.

For many, this can be the hardest part. If you are struggling with self-respect or self-esteem issues, you might need professional help to deal with these things so that you can become stable and healthy as an individual before becoming part of a couple.

Let go of baggage from previous relationships. Or at least get a firm handle on it so that it doesn't seep into your next relationship.

This is, obviously, easier said than done. Almost every relationship leaves us with a little baggage. Some of that baggage is actually helpful, as it can give us a clearer picture of what we do and don't want from a relationship. However, some of that baggage can be very detrimental. It might come from past romantic relationships but it might come from other past experiences as well.

If you have relationship baggage that makes you reactive, suspicious, afraid of intimacy or unsure about how a healthy relationship should look, it's time to figure out how to let those things go. The baggage might not be your fault, but you have to take ownership of the fact that you're holding onto it before you can become more centered, and either move on without it or learn to compartmentalize it in a way that doesn't control you as a person or how you handle new relationships.

Many people might need professional help with this process, especially if they have been physically, sexually or emotionally abused or sexually assaulted in the past. Don't let your abuser control your future. Take charge of your own life, starting now, and don't be ashamed to reach out for help.

What if rebounds help me forget about my ex so that I can take all these steps?

If a casual, rebound fling helps you get your ex off your mind, that's fine. Just remember that the goal is to spend time alone, so be cautious about this if you don't think you can keep it casual.

When we rebound, we have a tendency to do one of two things (though rebounds don't always follow these patterns): we either go for the same "type" every time, which often leads us to repeat the same mistakes from our last relationship, or we go for someone who is the complete opposite of our ex. Going for a certain "type" often leads us to someone who is too similar to our ex and has a lot of the qualities that the ex-had, which didn't work out for us the last time and probably won't be any different the next time. Going for someone who is the complete opposite can be equally problematic because we can end up yo-yoing between two different extremes when we really need a person with a more balanced personality.

Remember, when the last relationship just ended, we're usually not seeing the next person we meet clearly, so don't let those rose-colored rebound lenses lead you into another bad, or less than ideal, relationship. You deserve better than that.

What if I think I've met Mr./Ms. Right?

Take your time to really get to know them. If the person you just met is truly right for you, they will still be right for you in six months or a year. Where are you in the process we've just discussed? If your last relationship just ended yesterday, it's probably really hard to see the new person clearly. If you think they could be right for you in the future, that's all the more reason not to get involved right now and wait until you're ready.

If you've really worked through some of this process, you might be able to spend time with this person and take things really slowly until you've completed the process. If they are truly the right person, they will understand why you need to move slowly.

Even if you've completed this process and you're ready for the next relationship, still move slowly. Take the time to really get to know them over a period of time. Get to know who they are when they're no longer trying as hard to impress you. Get to know how they are in different situations and with different people. Get to know who they are on their bad days as well as their good days. Make sure you really know this person inside and out before you get too emotionally attached. Once you're attached, it's very hard to sever ties if you realize the person isn't good for you so really get to know them first.

When kids are involved

It's hard enough for adults to navigate through relationships, breakups and divorces. Imagine how hard it is on kids who don't have the coping tools and emotional maturity that adults have. Further, kids' sense of self and their concept of relationships is still developing.

When kids experience people coming in and out of their lives all the time, it's stressful, confusing and very destabilizing. It can lead to anxiety, depression, low self-esteem, emotional eating, separation anxiety, lack of trust, a sense of insecurity and feeling unsupported. Plus, the relationships they see now will affect their ability to have healthy, stable relationships later in life, so make sure you're in a healthy, stable relationship before your kids get to be a part of it.

As a rule of thumb, if you've just gone through a divorce or major breakup (basically, if the partner was involved in your kids' lives in any way), don't introduce your kids to your next romantic partner for at least a year. Even if you don't realize it, your kids get attached to the people you date and it's just as hard on them as it is on you when that person is lo longer in your lives, and maybe harder. Give your kids a chance to move on before exposing them to another person.

Regardless of how long it's been since your last relationship ended; don't introduce your partner into your kids' lives unless you really believe that the relationship will last in the long term. Remember, your kids will get attached to this person, so think hard about whether they will stay in your kids' lives for a very long time or if your kids will end up losing this person. When relationships end, you might see it as good riddance, but it can be very traumatic for you kids if they have gotten attached.

There are a lot of scumbags out there I won't lie, and choosing to only accept someone that passes all your requirements, can and will be difficult, but just think about it this way, when you do find someone that meets your expectations for yourself, you will have entered into a long and lasting partnership with someone who truly values you as much as you value yourself.

And in the meantime, you will have a better understanding and feeling about yourself, knowing that you are a valuable person, which is most defiantly going to make your single status a truly empowering place to be. When we feel empowered and confident we feel happiness. Take the time in your singleness to relate to yourself, to nurture yourself and to love yourself, and you will find happiness greater than any relationship, because you created it within yourself and it resides deep inside you, and no one can take it away!

CHAPTER 2

GET TO KNOW YOURSELF (DATE YOURSELF)

Being single, too many people are scary. I wonder why. When many people know that I am still single at the ripe old age of 32, they look at me as if i have cancer or AIDS and tell me that I must have really high expectations. They tell me if I do not want to be left on the shelf I should be less picky. I have been single for the past 4 years and still counting. Although there are times when I wish I had someone to lean on, like when I am ill or when I had an especially hard day at work, I see for myself that the advantages of being single far outweighs the friction that being part of a couple can cause. When I tell people that I enjoy being single, they think I am trying hard to put up a false front. They tell me that I should be out there dating. The truth is, many do not know I always have a hot date at hand.. Myself. No I am not out of my mind. A few years back after the most recent breakup, I realized that there isn't a year I had spent time being alone by myself and not getting involved in couple quarrels. I felt that I had been trying to find happiness from people around me. I expected them to give me happiness. And yet at the same time, I could not give them true happiness. How could I, when i can't even find happiness within myself? I knew I tried to please as many people as possible but I realize that I was even more unhappy at the end of the day. So that defeats the purpose of my actions which were supposed to make me happy in the first place.

I had to know myself first. So i spent time being alone, dating no one except myself and occasionally one or two girlfriends. But mostly by myself. I rediscover my strengths and weakness, what I look good in and what I don't. What is acceptable to me, what isn't? All this while being honest to myself. Being by myself gives me time to think and to physically remove myself from the crowd. It makes me feel better and understands myself more. I reassessed my past relationships and find out the root of the problems. I asked myself why I fell for guy A,B,C. I found out that I had wanted to feel loved and didn't want to be left alone to face the situation I was in. I thought I could find my knight in shining armor to rescue me from my situation but I was so wrong. I had to learn to walk out of my situation before dragging someone else in it.

People tend to change to accommodate their partners when they have one. It's not always good or bad but a relationship should not only be about the other person. It should be about two people growing together, being able to brave the storms and obstacles. It's not only about being accommodating. Both should take turns making decisions and being the leader. It's definitely hard to be in a relationship and even harder to keep it going.

I am not condemning relationships over here. Deep down I do want to be loved too. But he has to be someone who understands me and love me the way that is appropriate for me and not what he thinks should be. He should be able to draw a balance, knowing when to do what. In short, someone very wise and loves me a lot and yet lets me have my private times by myself. Hard to find? You bet.

There is nothing more greater than someone who is happy, self-assured, busy, and fulfilled. Whether you are in a relationship or not, it is extremely important to continue to nurture yourself with all of the wonderful things that usually accompany a new relationship. Everyone has experienced a time in their lives when they have received flowers either at work or at the start of a date. For some reason, this simple gesture can make you feel so special and loved. I realized that you don't need a man in your life to achieve these same feelings. I will give you many examples of how to do this, but, in general, remember to find the practices that make you feel good and build your self-confidence.

The first practice I developed in dating yourself is a romantic evening. When things in life get busy or stressful, schedule yourself a dinner. Make sure you buy everything you would if you were preparing a meal for a significant other such as candles, a nice bottle of wine, and a decadent dessert. Spa dates are another great way to pamper yourself. The key here, just as it was with the romantic dinner, is to create the same environment you would if you were preparing a romantic bath for your lover. Writing a love letter to yourself is another great tool in dating yourself. This is a simple practice that, when done regularly, can remind you what an amazing person you are and how much you deserve to be loved.

Pink! It is really important that you have many different items in both your environment and your wardrobe that make you feel feminine. When I wear pink I notice an immediate difference in the way I feel. Another great bonus of wearing pink is that I receive compliments daily. The color of your clothes is a little thing that can make a big difference. Getting dressed up just as you would for a date is another practice that I highly recommend in dating yourself. This is especially important when you are single; it can help you attract people into your life. There is truth in the saying, "You look good, you feel good." Make sure to take extra time primping your hair and applying makeup. Spending extra time and energy making yourself look and feel good, will cause you to radiate a different energy than usual. Sexy lingerie is a must when you are dating yourself. I believe that lingerie is just as much for yourself as it is for your partner, if not more. Here is a little challenge for you: I encourage you to wear sexy lingerie every day for a week under your regular clothes. I guarantee you that this alone will give you a whole different perception of yourself, and it will give off a different energy to others.

Dating myself has taught me many things. It tells me who my real friends are. Who really cares and who doesn't. What's really important to me and what isn't? It made me think about what I want in someone and because I am not in a hurry to give up my single status, I will observe and analyses and ponder and not leap before looking. I feel that a real relationship, whether it's with a friend or lover, is about finding someone who brings out the best in you, enjoys the best in you and loves you for the things you love.

CHAPTER 3

LOVE YOURSELF

I believe there are two types of people in this world: those who look before they leap and those who leap before they look. "Leaping before looking" can create results in one of two ways. On the one hand, it can prove you to be courageous and brave. On the other hand, it can cause you to get in a bit over your head at times.

The key to attracting the love that you want in your life is to love yourself first. Not just to say it, but to mean it, to feel it, to actually and truly sincerely love yourself. The greatest part is that this is also the secret to attracting anything else you desire in your life. It starts with you first.

Its principle is to cultivate the Sanskrit word metta, which means "love" or "loving kindness," into our lives. The true definition of metta is kind, unconditional well-wishing. It is an open-hearted nurturing of ourselves and others: accepting ourselves and others just as we (and they) are, rather than for how we would want them to be.

Break-ups have always been the main cause of heartbreaks and bitterness among some of us. It is the start of demise spirits, impetuous crazy acts, and unreasonable decisions. In breaking-up with an important person, one's being is also being busted. Why a lot of us are holding on to the very last ounce of probability there is, "to save our relationship with our partners though we are hurt in the process?", but as long as love and respect still exist in your relationship, the whole thing is worth mending, but the real question is, after all the odds, after all the callous and heartless words, as well as ruthless remarks, after all the tears have fallen, and black-and-blue spirit, what's left to patch up?

Love is about forbearing and continuing pain for the sake of loving someone, the idea of mending relationships boils down to the reality that we all treasure our relationship, and is willing to fight for it up to the last end. It is very easy to say than done, saving your breaking relationship is an annoying, and wearing experience. The physical pain you feel is as hurting as your emotions involved. It generates a global of madness in your mind. Mending your relationship is indeed a step-by-step process that involves coherent thinking. Here are great tips in mending your broken heart.

-The very first thing to bear in mind is that both of you should accept the fact that there is really a problem that exist in your relationship. Some of us rebuff to face it. We tend to avoid the issue because we are scared that the person we love will ultimately be gone for good. That manner is very bad one and it doesn't help at all. If you will just accept the fact that there is a problem, it makes the mending course easier.

-By giving space, it doesn't inevitably follow that both will leave the relationship. Give each other some time to cool your heads both and recuperate thoughts. In this manner you'll miss each other's company.

Relationship is composed of two different people, and not by just a lone individual. In order to make the relationship flourish, a good joint venture between the two of you should be observed. Both should be functioning out together. In a relationship, it is a give-and-take method. Sacrifices are drawn in if you really want to keep, and continue your relationship. You have to do definite things for your loved one even though you are not used to. These things are very simple, yet may hold much bearing to your love one. Love all the time. Others may consider love as a hyped topic, but it is reason why many relationships have withstood all trials and struggles that tried destroying the relationship. As long as love is present for each other, your relationship is worth staying. Mending a relationship needs sacrifices, persistence, patience and a stable heart. A trial really exists, and strikes anytime, through this, it is either your relationships are busted or strengthened. You should bear in mind that along this process of mending relationship, you should not forget yourself, because of too much love and extreme anxiety to fix broken portions, we tend to disregard that we have also the obligation to love ourselves.

How To Love Yourself Through Heartbreak and Grief

You can take the following steps to love yourself and manage pain with both past and current pain.

Put your hands on your chest, breathing into your heart and inviting the spiritual presence of love and compassion into your heart.

Let your inner child - your feeling self - know that you understand that he or she is feeling the deep pain of heartbreak or grief, that you are here with him or her and you are not going to leave him or her alone with the pain. You are going to love yourself through it rather than continue to abandon yourself.

Stay lovingly and compassionately fully present with the pain until you feel it start to release. Once it subsides, then gives it to Spirit and ask for inner peace.

Open to learning with your higher self about any information you need about the situation causing the pain, and about what action would be loving to yourself.

Take whatever loving action you are guided to take.

Go back inside to see how you are feeling now. Hopefully, you are feeling some relief.

Do this each time the same pain or pain from a different situation comes up. With big losses and other very painful situations, the pain might come up over and over, and in order to not continue to abandon yourself, you need to lovingly manage the pain each time. You can do this same process to release past pain.

We spend our whole life in search of love from others. We wish that true love will find us and that special love will change our life. If you don't find the love then you fall into the valley of emptiness and feel lost. We always tell our mind that if I get true love then I will be the happiest person on the earth. Actually it works the other way round. You need to love yourself to get love from others and you need to love yourself to give love to others. 2

CHAPTER 4

STAY COMMITTED TO YOURSELF

Mindset and attitude are so important in determining your success in anything you want to achieve. But, what does that really mean for us. First, we want to look at what we do daily in terms of feeding our minds. What type of information do you feed your mind with? Do you read daily inspirational things? Are you listing to self-development audio? If you are not feeding your mind daily with positive information please do this for yourself. This will give you the strength to go through your process in attaining your goal. Also, what is your attitude about your goal? Do you believe in yourself that you can really achieve this goal or, do you have internal self-doubt? You must have full confidence in your abilities to achieve success in anything you want to succeed in. You must not doubt yourself in your ability to get what you want. Self-confidence comes when we start to see results in our goals however, we must first have a good mindset by feeding our minds daily, mediating and visualizing ourselves with whatever it is we desire.

It is so tempting to open yourself up to another person before you're truly content and aware of who you are as a person. Maybe your friends are in relationships, maybe you're feeling lonely and would give anything to have someone to love. All you want is to have a hand to hold and a shoulder to cry on, but if you aren't ready, it will more than likely lead to heartbreak like no other.

Before you commit yourself to someone else, take time, whether it be months or years, to figure yourself out. Read books, discover good music, align your political views, figure out your sense of style. Get to know yourself incredibly well; become your own best friend. Learn to be comfortable in your own skin and love yourself. This last step is undoubtedly the hardest, but with time and proper self-exploration, it will come.

Becoming your own unique person and learning to be content with that person is when you know for sure who you want to be surrounded by. You'll be able to seek out friends who complement your personality and you'll be able to find a person who is good for you to open up to.

I made the mistake of diving into the world of relationships too soon. I was not comfortable or confident, and all I wanted was to feel like I belonged. I wasted my time and I got my heart broken. I wish more than anything that I would have waited, because the person I am today is a person I am proud to be, and I am with someone who is just as proud of whom I am.

Don't rush in and certainly don't settle. Spend time growing and becoming yourself. There is no one else quite likes you, and once you come to that realization; the world (and the people in it) is your oyster.

It is impossible to experience true intimacy with another if we are ignoring the needs of our own heart. How can we truly be with someone if we are avoiding ourselves?

So often in our intimate relationships, we are focused on what the other will provide in terms of emotional support. It is easy to point the finger, blame them for being disappointing and letting us down. Yet, are we willing to commit to ourselves?

Life is short and fragile, and we never know whether today is our last day. Bringing ourselves deeply back into our hearts allows us to choose our next steps from a place of self-love.

Close your eyes, breathe deeply, and ask yourself this important question: "What do I most need from me right now?"

It can take time to recover from the end of a long-term relationship and readjust to these life changes. I spent a long time processing painful emotions that arose and sadness I felt while adjusting.

There was deep self-reflection, even resulting in spending time at a retreat in Brazil. I stripped my life back to the bare essentials, withdrew from much socializing for a long time, and began to reacquaint myself with myself. I began to reinvest in the relationship with my own heart rather than seeking love from someone else's.

The more we nourish ourselves, the more able we are to share this love with others from a place of surplus and not deficit. This brings such freedom and joy, both to us and others. Is it time for you to commit to yourself.

CHAPTER 5

FIND YOUR PURPOSE

"Sometimes things fall apart so that better things can fall together." ~Marilyn Monroe

Whether we're processing disappointment or a tragedy, heartache can seem irrevocable, as if our entire existence has been nuked into bleak devastation.

While it can be hard to consider the possibility that these barren circumstances could be necessary, or fruitful, heartbreak can show us a great inner strength that exists in unsuspecting, subtle ways.

I was never the kind of person who was convinced that consuming, true love was real. (You know the kind that Celine Dion sings about.) Yet, that is exactly where I found myself when I met a man who had a set of traits that I had only dreamed of.

And when it abruptly ended, with no explanation, I was devastated and bewildered. Now on the other side, these are the things I would have said to the girl laying on the pitch-black bathroom floor when she was drowning in questions about faith and forgiveness.

Every activity is an act of strength when you're struggling.

Every time you get out of bed, go to a yoga class, or just do the dishes is a strong initiative of willpower because you're pushing forward with your life, household, and health. You may still feel depressed, but it's in these small measures that you're seeding something wholesome for your present and future.

Be proud you took a risk.

While the destination may not be the oasis you'd envisioned, you have to remember why you set out on the journey.

You took a chance by opening up to someone or attempting a new endeavor. It takes a great deal of courage to venture into an exploration of the precarious unknown, and you have to give yourself praise for making an effort.

Move with the emotion.

Sorrow can feel like a suffocating place of confinement. Yet trying to power through and forcing yourself to get over what you're feeling is an act of denial. Our sentiments are a part of us and they can't be amputated on command. Honor this part of yourself and try to progress with it in tow.

Accept your choices.

We can incessantly pick at the "should haves" and "would haves," but your inner GPS chose a route based on the information you had at the time. You couldn't have done anything different. When you can fully embrace this, it is an act of forgiveness to yourself, because you stop questioning your capabilities. Everything you did was as it was supposed to be.

Stay present.

The monkey mind wants to pick at the past and guess about the future. It takes work, but when you can fully focus on the details of the present moment, the questions and concerns will subside. You can do this by taking notice of your senses in your immediate surroundings—the taste, smell, touch, and of course your breath.

Just like any fitness routine, it takes practice. Don't be bothered by the number of times you have to re-center your thoughts; just keep doing it.

Look for beauty.

Whether you go to a museum, a botanical garden, or just enjoy a sunset, seek out the aesthetic that you find pleasing. Doing so will allow you to reconnect with a part of your true self. It can also be a soothing reminder that there are other amazing things in life beyond your distressed situation.

Knowing your life purpose creates more intimate, fulfilling, and balanced relationships. This is true if you if you are single (or single again) and are planning to be in a relationship after a break up

Life purpose answers the questions of, "Who am I?", and, "Why am I here?". This knowledge and insight creates a firm foundation for you to build your life on.

This is much like the foundation of a house. When a house is built on a solid foundation, the house stands solid, withstanding numerous conditions.

When you know your life purpose you know what you value, you know what is important, and therefore, what isn't important as well. You have far fewer power struggles, less room for dependency, and when you and your life-partner both know your corresponding life purpose; the relationship becomes a very sacred space that supports both of you in your life journey.

If you are single or just having hard times from heartbreak, knowing your life purpose is one the most important elements in making effective relationship choices. You will want someone who fits into your purpose, and who can support and understand it.

Likewise, it is wise to be with someone who has a life purpose of their own. In knowing your life purpose you define yourself through it, rather than through the relationship or through the other person. You know who you are, where you are going, what is important, and what you are looking for.

Without knowing your life purpose you have a higher likelihood of choosing out of fear and dependency, and thereby, settling for a relationship that is not in your best interest.

Knowing your life purpose may be the most powerful element in creating and continuing in healthy and sustaining relationships

CHAPTER 6

EXERCISE TO FEEL GOOD

Almost everyone views heartbreak as an emotional problem. So how precisely will exercise help you if you are suffering emotionally?

Most people do not recognize the mind-body connection. Our minds and bodies are connected in the way we respond to stress and emotional pain. Any stress you feel in your mind, you also will feel in your body. Any stress you feel in your body, you will definitely feel in your mind. No doubt about it.

Exercise is one of the simplest ways to help in mending a broken heart. Exercise allows you to release all of that tension in your body and pumps your brain with endorphins. Besides that, exercise also helps you to shed any unwanted pounds and aids in shaping your physical appearance. This will enable you to boost your confidence and makes you feel good about yourself.

If you've recently experienced heartache, you might have wanted to immediately turn to a tub of ice cream and Netflix to mend a broken heart. We've all been there. I've been there. But guess what? While you might feel temporary pleasure from burrowing under the covers and eating high-fat, high-sugar, high-calorie snacks, you are actually digging yourself into a deeper hole than before – forgoing more long-term happiness.

By remaining inactive not only will your heart be aching, but you will generally feel more lethargic, tired and bloated. Wouldn't it be better to deal with the emotional hurt while feeling physically fit? It's seriously one less problem to think about.

Not only this, but "giving up" on working out oftentimes leads to poorer eating habits which then becomes a never-ending cycle. You don't work out, so you eat poorly, the next day you feel gross (not to mention, sad) and don't work out again and …. before you know it not only are you feeling bad about someone "rejecting" you, but you are also rejecting yourself because you know you could feel and look better with just a little bit of effort.

Of course, everyone should love their body first and foremost at whatever stage it's at, but that feeling after a grueling workout that you didn't give up on? That feeling after even just a week of staying on your grind? That feeling of strutting your stuff because you feel good in your own skin? That's confidence. While some boy/girl's actions towards you may have given your self-esteem a shot, working out regularly can mend that wound and probably quicker than you think. This boost from hitting the gym will help you bounce back, feel good about yourself and mend that broken heart so you're not stuck wallowing.

Not only that, but exercise busies the mind. Whether your workout is 10 minutes, 15 minutes a day or 30 minutes, it helps you get your mind off things. Why? Time flies and you're probably too busy thinking about keeping up or not passing out to think about Mr. or Mrs. So-and-so – or who I like to call "Irrelevant". If you're working out regularly, it's even better. It's essential to have hobbies you can dedicate yourself whole-heartedly to.

What Exercise Can Do For Your Heartbreak

You're hurting emotionally and most likely don't want to leave your bedroom. What can exercise really do to relieve the pain you feel right now?

How Exercise Helps Mend Your Broken Heart:

- Exercise helps you fight depression.
- Exercise gives you energy.
- Exercise helps your brain produce those "feel-good" hormones.
- Exercise allows you to be more social.
- Exercise boosts your confidence.
- Exercise allows your brain to deal with stress better.

These benefits of exercise are good for your overall health and emotional well-being. The greatest benefit of exercise is that it makes you look better. When you look better, you feel better. When you feel better, you do better. Exercise is one of the fastest ways to improve your looks, overall health, and spirit. Your clothes will fit better. Your confidence will skyrocket. People in your inner circle will start to notice the improvement in your body and compliment you. Your heartbreak will seem insignificant, and you will begin to move on.

My Experience with Exercise after A Broken Heart

After my break up, exercising was the last thing on my mind. I really wanted to stay in bed as much as I possibly could. Eventually, I started to get back into my routine and workout regularly again. I also started eating better, not really overdoing it, but just watching what I ate and took better care of myself. Before I knew it, I had lost about 20 lbs in a little less than 2 months.

I will never forget when I first saw my ex some months after our break up. The expression on his face said it all. He was shocked to see how good I looked. 20 lbs is a lot of weight to lose and makes a great difference in your appearance. I felt so powerful and confident knowing that I had improved myself and made my ex feel like a fool for dumping me. I also felt great when all of a sudden men were approaching me left and right. My confidence shined through, and that really helped me move on after my break up.

Mending a broken heart can be taxing on your body. Exercise is one of the best ways to fight that stress and release all of those unwanted emotions that have been building up since your break up.

You don't have to start off with strenuous exercise. You can start off by taking a walk around the block for 20 minutes. Start with something small and build your way up. No one said that you had to mend your broken heart in one exercise session.

Remember, this about making you feel good as fast as possible. Trust me, just the sheer feeling of getting out and moving around will make a huge difference in the way you feel right now. So, get up and get moving!

CHAPTER 7

LEARN NEW SKILL

Do you see your ex's name everywhere you look? Do the smallest things, even the most mundane objects, remind you of him or her? This happens because so much of our experiences are linked with that other person. However, when we learn new things, we get to have brand new experiences that are completely our own. Learning a new language, for example, gives your mind too much of a cognitive load to continue being focused on memories of an ex. Open yourself up to new languages, people, and cultures. Make the world feel a little bigger.

Even if learning a new language isn't for you, consider other things you would like to take on like a pottery class, wine tasting club, or gym membership. Choose a class that lasts six weeks, so that it becomes built in to your schedule and provides you with the chance to get to know new people over time. When we learn new things we achieve a sense of progress and self-improvement that counteract false feelings of rejection or failure that sometimes accompany breakups.

Whatever the skill we should all ensure that we are learning every day until we get over any sort of heartbreak depression. Jimmy Gould became depressed as his 50th birthday approached and his counselor suggested that he learn three skills - along with another person if possible. First he persuaded a friend that they should improve their English language skills. The plan was to read slowly through a good book and write

43

down phrases that caught their attention. At their weekly meeting they would practice using the phrases until they became very familiar. They chose a book from Jimmy's bookcase called the Matter of Wales by Jan Morris and within minutes they wrote down and rehearsed the following phrases: repositories of old folk wisdom, his voice was curiously beguiling, a wonderfully percipient man, it was comically apt, he felt something ominous in the air, spindrifts of spray flying helter-skelter over the heather, the ferocious tide.

They role played a conversation with these phrases used in an appropriate context. By changing books every few weeks they practiced a large number of diverse phrases and words that slowly became part of their everyday language. As a second learning mission Jimmy walked through his local woods three times each week and with the help of the internet he got to know the name of every tree on his route. The third skill was learning the flute thanks to a 26 year old woman who lived locally. After 6 months Jimmy's depression scores had plummeted and were down to within the normal range.

With the surge of adrenaline and cortisol that you get after a break up telling you to get up and get out (aka numb yourself to the pain by partying and hooking up with others) you have a huge opportunity.

Get your exercise routine dialed, learn a new skill, or build a new business.

I have had clients who built successful seven figure businesses from the surge of adrenaline that they got from an especially painful breakup.

Some of the best art in the world was made by people who had lost love. Utilize this current of emotional energy for your personal gain.

CHAPTER 8

TRAVEL

We have all had a broken heart; have felt that intoxicating rush of falling in love only to be followed by the exquisite pain of realizing it was a mirage. How one maneuvers the choppy waves of heartbreak differs; some turn towards friends, others seek solace in loneliness, while many choose to travel.

Breakups—we've all been there—a time of distress, anxiety, misery, maybe nostalgic tears over a bowl of ice cream. I'm all for mourning a relationship, whether it's a mutual split or heartache, but there comes a time when you are ready to move on.

One of the best ways to get out there again is to take a trip—anywhere—to clear your mind, restore your self-confidence, get out into the world, and use your newfound independence as a chance to grow.

Instead of wallowing in self-pity and obsessive thoughts about what might have been, hit the road.

Travel is a sure catharsis, as it removes you from familiar surroundings, from the apartment you shared and from all the friends you had in common. The risk to bump into an ex at your favorite watering hole is reduced to zero. Distance creates a space in which you can begin to refocus.

By traveling, you're thrust into the unfamiliar, and out of your comfort zone. It's liberating to be in a place where no one knows your name and are able to give yourself a break and get out of your head for a bit.

You can also take this chance to learn something new on your travels. Want to try your hand at photography? Start by taking pictures of the huge world. Took Spanish in college? Try out what you remember in a local restaurant. Start doing yoga. Volunteer while you're abroad. The limit is only your imagination.

Travel is said to be the cure-all for a broken heart – the quickest way to step above the rising waters of sorrow and find the strength to move forward.

A broken heart heals with time. It does not matter if your heart is broken from a relationship, a personal lost, a divorce, unfair treatment or stress from unfair treatment. There is one cure that even the Medical Doctors agree on; "Travel" During your travels your heart will encounter the necessary people, emotions, experiences and events to help you heal more quickly.

The first thing you must do is select a destination that you have always wanted to visit. It does not matter that you don't feel like going, just do it! Go to the Caribbean, Hawaii or Mexico and sit on the beach all day for 5 or 6 days or until you feel life again.

At this point we must explore a "correct" travel plan vs. an "incorrect" travel plan. A "correct" travel plan to help mend a broken heart would include unpacking only once for the duration of the trip. It would also include an easy arrival and departure from your destination. Non-stop flight, express pick-up from the airport, express check-in at the hotel, excellent room service, warm weather, beach hut, white sandy beach OR a 5 to 7 day cruise (warm weather)

Sitting on the beach all day (under the little hut) for 3 to 7 days will definitely help with your emotional status, It is something about the sound of the ocean that is energizing, calming and memorable. Be prepared to cry, this will ensure you that your spirit is still alive.

Do what feels good, every day. The memories you make of your trip will stay with you always and remind you who you are and what you can do, just by yourself.

CHAPTER 9

SAVE AND MAKE MORE MONEY

Another excellent way to get over your ex is to channel your energy towards building a stronger financial fortress. Making some more money and have some extra cash stacked away in your bank account can give you some good feel and security which is necessary when trying to get over the bad feelings that come with heartbreak.

One may ask, "How do I save and make more money?" The answer is not far-fetched and is unveiled in a few lines below.

From the very beginning when human beings started money to trade and barter for goods and services, they have also searched for new methods to increase the amount of money in their possession. This search has in many ways inspired one of the classic human questions: How do I make more money for myself, or how do I make the money that I have gone further? While it's certainly possible to get a new job, sell all of your possessions, or take out a loan, for most people, the best way to make more money is to save more of the money that you already make.

Most people focus on the fact this strategy for making your money do more does mean that you're not going to have as much money to spend right now. However, if you do everything right, eventually there will be enough to cover you if things go south or you want to treat yourself to something beautiful.

Furthermore, the truth is that saving money isn't more difficult than most other things; it only takes a little commitment, careful planning, and the self-control to make yourself stick to your plan.

Your most important and potentially only course of action when trying to save money is to take an inventory of all your current costs. There's a lot of ways to do this, but one of the most efficient methods is to every purchase you prepare for a week. You can do this on your phone, or you can carry around a small notebook to track your purchases and expenses. At the end of the week takes out your list of purchases and see what it looks like. There are possibilities that you will find a lot of purchases on that list that weren't mandatory and didn't need to be made. Once you add up all the gum, coffee, and meals out, you'll realize that there are plenty of easy ways to save money. For example, make your coffee at home before work instead of buying it from Starbucks for $3. Cut back on those expensive dinners out and cook at home for a fraction of the price. If it looks like you're spending too much money on gas to get to and from work, then consider looking into mass transit if it is available where you live. Maybe you could even use some of that money to buy yourself a bike and begin a whole new, healthier daily commute.

The apparent truth is that most of us spend more money than we need to on things that we don't need. You will probably be amazed by what you find on your spending inventory and all the things that might leave you perplexed and with a scratchy head. Bottom line: If you take a closer look at your spending today, it is guaranteed that you will find easy ways to save. After all, it's always worth your time to find out what kind of money you could be keeping in your bank account.

When you find yourself battling to get over your Ex, taking to making more money and saving doesn't only keep you busy and make you think less of memories, it has a way of giving you excellent and fulfilling feelings that energizes you for tomorrow.

CHAPTER 10

SPEND MORE TIME WITH FAMILY AND FRIENDS

"Spending time with family and friends" is outlined last, but it is not the least. In fact, I consciously placed it here because it is considered as the most important.

Family and Friends; which I refer to as the "Two Fs" are life's greatest treasures you can ever have; whether heartbroken or at any other time. Never lose sight of them!

When battling to get over the memories of an Ex, the best approach is to get closer to loved ones who are often present when they are most needed.

The story below will make you understand better: His fiancé once dumped a friend. He was physically shaken and devastated. I still remember the day when I picked him up from the park and drove him back to his mother's place. When she got the clue of what happened, she was practically helpful with words and made us a nice cup of tea.

The siblings were happy to see their brother after a long while. They had no clue that their brother was going through heartbreak. The following six months were excruciating; living lonely without a partner, feeling hopeless, depressed and lost. The lady was gone, so were his happiness and the memories they shared. Only two things remained unchanged - Family and Friends. With their support and encouragement, he got into another relationship within six months. Today, he's enjoying a better relationship, so is his happiness, but the bonding with the "2Fs" has grown even stronger. No matter what is lost, family and friends should and will last forever.

Few tips that will help you bond better with family and friends:

1. Consciously make out time to be with family and friends. Set aside an additional half hour every day, to sit with the family and do something everybody likes (TV, a chat or a board game).

2. Be present and eat meals together with your family.

3. Try your best to wake up with a smile. It radiates down to the whole family.

4. Never set your expectations too high and do not forget to appreciate your family and friends for all the good that they do for you.

5. Finding a service project to do is also a fantastic idea for some family togetherness. Perhaps an older neighbor needs help with the leaves or snow. Or a local library needs help shelving books. Maybe a shelter needs assistance handing out food and other essentials. Not only will your family be together. They will leave feeling lucky to have one another all they have.

6. Doing an activity is another good way to get to enjoy moments with your family members. The above might include raking leaves or painting a room or shoveling snow. Even doing dishes or cooking are great ways to enjoy moments with family members. These activities are especially useful because they have many different levels of difficulty in them. For instance,

when cooking, little children can stir while older ones chop and slice meats and vegetables. Even doing a craft activity is a great idea. It gets everyone around timetable doing the same thing.

Getting yourself braced with the above will give you happiness in abundance and the required energy to get over the haunting memories of your Ex. The above is an essential step towards self-help - a happier and better you!

In conclusion, when trying to get over your Ex, learn to value yourself and be attentive to how others treat you which includes family members and friends. Avoid gatherings, people or events that do not make you feel good. It is important to note that you are not responsible for the way others think or behave. Pay particular attention to your family connections. If you succumb to other's control or manipulations, you become an enabler of their behavior. Make sure your self-talk is as though you are talking to your favorite person on the planet. Learn to love yourself completely!

CONCLUSION

Battling with different issues after a break up like getting over your ex is a common ordeal for many lovers who ended up in separate ways. Detaching yourself from the emotions you have for your ex needs a lot of perseverance and self-control. When you make the wrong choices and decisions you end up being trapped in your past, living a miserable life.

Lots of people may give you well meant advice. And although a lot of it maybe good, this advice can also be very wrong. This advice is most of the time meant to heal things up again. Like trying to tell her you are sorry, giving her presents and so on. Sometimes this can be good but now let's see it from the other side. Let's start with my one great tip to get over your ex: Time heals all wounds.

This does not mean you sit back on your lazy..., do nothing and hope it will pass as fast as possible. No, that is not the way it works. You should take this as a great opportunity to search out some old friends, pick up some long forgotten hobby or a new one, and start working on your shape like you were thinking to do for a few years now. Those kinds of things will help you in getting over that ex. In other words try to build up your life again. Go out there and meet new people, do new things and live your BEST LIFE!!

Please leave a review on Amazon to help me promote my book because I don't have the big marketing machines like some of the big book publishers companies to promote this book ..If you find this book to be helpful please share with a family member or a friend ..

Thanks , Madison and Lamont

For more information on upcoming free books email me your email address at

lamontholliday@gmail.com

Made in the
USA
Monee, IL

14541810R00035